A Curious Mix
in free verse

WATTLETALES
PUBLISHING

Lindy Warrell

WATTLETALES
PUBLISHING

Published by Wattletales Publishing
Adelaide, Australia
https://www.wattletales.com.au

First published by Wattletales Publishing in 2022.

Copyright © Lindy Warrell
The moral right of the author has been asserted.

Except as permitted by the Australian Copyright Act 1968, no part of this book may be reproduced, stored in a retrieval system, or transmitted for or by any means, electronic, mechanical, photocopying recording, or otherwise, without prior permission from the copyright owner and the publisher of this book.

Wattletales Publishing and the author acknowledge that this book was written on the lands of the Kaurna people, traditional owners of the Adelaide Plains, and pay respect to their Elders past, present and emerging.

Cover Design and Typesetting: Nicola Matthews, Nikki Jane Design, Canberra

ISBN: 978-0-6453129-2-8 (Paperback)
ISBN: 978-0-6453129-3-5 (eBook)

Cataloguing-in-Publication entry is available
From the National Library of Australia
https://catalogue.nla.gov.au

This mix of free verse is like the random jam of a jazz band, it makes you listen, smile and feel the rhythms of humanity. An anthropologist, Lindy Warrell is a keen observer of people; with apt imagery and sharp wit, she captures a familiar world. Warrell's poems take you to the truth of trees, to lusty youth and the not-so-funny joke of old age. Rich and bold as a golden sax, Warrell's poems celebrate strong women, ancestors, birds and wildlife, and the gift of being alive. These memorable, no-holds-barred poems resonate long after reading.

Jude Aquilina

This is a superbly constructed anthology of free verse which challenges and is seared with examples of human vulnerability, along with humour, dark moments and tender insight. There's much to enjoy and savour in Lindy Warrell's *A Curious Mix of Free Verse*, not least in concluding lines such as — *we'd probably die out if we were potatoes* — and a telling summation of how *we glow in the sunshine of love*. Lindy has the poet's true instinct of recording impressions wherever she finds herself.

Roger Rees

*I dedicate this book to the splendidly permissive state of old age.
Those of us who get here are grateful.
To those on the way, enjoy.*

Contents

Contents	i-iii
Crushing the Magic	1
Nana in Sepia	2
A Poem Is	3
Questions of Sex	4
Bird Paintings	5
Wayward Storm	6
Black and White Song	7
Short Rumination on Politics	8
Those Were the Days	9
Abiding	10
As We Drive	11
Deception	12
An Unquiet Garden	13
As For Cats, Least Said...	14
Giving or Taking?	15
Along the Way	16
A Tale of Two Trees	17
Damaged Goods	18
Deconstruction	20
Desk Magic	21
At My Place	22
It Starts with Pink and Blue	23
Kintsugi	24
Iso in the City	25
The Shame	26
Emergency	27
Lazy Afternoons	28
Natural Selection?	29
Looking back	30
An Undecided Sky	31

Here I Am	32
Making the Bed	33
Keep Up Peeps	34
Serious Nonsense	36
My Poet	37
Navigation	38
Now You See It	39
On Visits	40
Old Age	41
Once Upon an Apple	42
Red	43
Over and Out	44
Seduction	45
Relentless	46
Of Eucalypts Lost	47
Relevance Deprivation	48
Oddments	49
Things	50
Sleep is a Faithless Lover	51
Silence	52
Plucking Day	53
Company of Strangers	54
Spring	56
Please Stop	57
Spent	58
Stillness	59
Coastal Fragments	60
Lost Words	61
Surrender	62
Freedom	63
The Desert Lies	64
Batik Bong	65
Startled	66
Wrong Killer	67
Smoke is Sublime	68

The Last Sausage	69
Back Then	70
Summer	72
Legacy in Sepia	73
The Missionary Position	74
At This Moment	75
My Telly Habit	76
Begone	77
To Exist	78
My First Husband	79
Sad Fact of Night	80
Where Truth Lies	81
Waiting	82
Till Wrinkles Come	83
Trees	84
To Wrack and Ruin	85
Today's Poem	86
Tourist Dreams	87
Water Most Fowl	88
Be Still	89
Willy Wagtail	90
Through Glass Blindly	91
Who Nicked the Sun?	92
Tinkle Time	93
The Time is Nigh	94

Acknowledgements
About the Author

A Curious Mix
in free verse

A Curious Mix in Free Verse

Crushing the Magic

Murmuration is reserved
for flocks of starlings,
So, I will be a susurration of leaf song.

By night, I'll croon to the moon
and spangle with stars
while rugged roots
anchor me deep in beloved earth.

Suddenly, I feel like a kaleidoscope,
an ineluctable mood
overwhelms me
of ever-changing colours,
shapes and sizes forming
and re-forming in oscillations
of crystal droplets, ruby slivers, and shiny black beads.

Lindy Warrell

Nana in Sepia

Nana, you, Nana
buttons, lots of buttons too tight
hair like a bird's nest
stiff, too stiff and pinned down
high ruffled collar choking
you, Nana, rigid in
buttons and frills
with three kids. Huh?
Wow. Must've had sex, Nana
but never smile
no smile, ever.

Not you, Nana, husband
drink drunk smashed head
on the mantelpiece
you, Nana, left with three kids
alone. Cold water flat
hungry, starving
no man wants a buttoned-up woman
with all those children.

A Curious Mix in Free Verse

A Poem Is

Can we see with words?
See-through them
or with them?

Is a poem a window
into life's heart
or a vulture that shreds flesh
into a million pieces of…

…of what?

Does reading a poem
reflect you back to yourself
or transport you elsewhere?
Is it not a mirror
that shivers to shards
as you gaze at yourself…

…nothing there?

Lindy Warrell

Questions of Sex

why does a man look sexy
naked above slacks
and pathetic in shirt and tie
above his hairy legs?

what is it about the suit mystique
that makes a girl see flannel
pyjamas with stripes erect
and cords all a-dangle?

is a woman more alluring
nude or in negligee?
does the drape of silk
seduce
or the writhe of satin sheets
arouse?
why do bare toes sticking out
bring us to giggles
when they wriggle in ecstasy?

do soft invitations
with tongues and moans
beat the hard-pressed
grind
on a dark dance floor?

Oh! Dear, I wish I could remember.

A Curious Mix in Free Verse

Bird Paintings

Sulphur-crested cockatoos and lorikeets
splotch the town canopy
in a chatter of springtime colour,
their black parrot cousins
shred fragrant pines, yellow tails
in shady beachside haunts.

Galahs flock to town
in summer
to dot paint the landscape
in a screech of pink and grey,
they nest and feast
then fly away.

Corellas repaint in white.

Lindy Warrell

Wayward Storm
(in the absence of 'e')

Plops of drops on fragrant pandanus
rain tinkling on tin
strumming on an old iron roof
dribbling down a window
lurking among curtains in my mind.

Wind songs roam through canopy,
a swaying whining church chorus that
wilts shrubs and blossoms in its downward chill.
I catch a sharp blast in my coat.
It saps my vitality.

Moon's hail plays blind golf
across front lawns, cars
roads and public parks
pot-shotting folk out and about.

Warm and dry in my room
I stay away from storm's wayward will
wood burns in an iron grid
its gift of warmth, my comfort and salvation.

A Curious Mix in Free Verse

Black and White Song

Sacred sparks
from little larks called Peewees
sprinkle the washing in back yards
fly above vast ochre plains
float in the haze of dry riverbeds
flit among blue-green swoops
of fragrant eucalypts
and flap wings in tropical forests,
their song uplifting the saddest heart.

Lindy Warrell

Short Rumination on Politics

Detached discourse
flickers of opinion
a mesmerising buzz of thought bubbles
inscribed
in a multi-media maze
pulsating through eyes and ears
to disturb hearts and minds
from the truth.

What's that? I hear you ask.

A Curious Mix in Free Verse

Those Were the Days

From beneath floppy straw brims
the silk bow of innocence peeks out
till the dresser fills with fascinators,
lover-attractors traded on Marketplace
for a modest wedding veil
whipped off by reality's veracity.

Mothering hair shines unadorned,
loose and soft
till glamour ends in grey streaks,
gardening hats, dirt-stained gloves
and sunblock.

Before long, we downgrade to joggers,
tracky-daks and sensible chemist-bought
sun-visors. When it's too hot or too cold
we go inside to pour over photos —
of the fascinators we left behind.

Lindy Warrell

Abiding

Earthly bed to my tree
roots spangling with fungi
singing to other trees
from dactyl
to canopy and beyond.

Let no one slice your trunk
nor make you bleed for me
or worse
dry your sap with fire —
too hot for you to renew.

I would bring you water
to quell disease
feed the future
but the river is dry
my tank is empty.

May tomorrow be luminous.

A Curious Mix in Free Verse

As We Drive

Morning sun glistens with promise
leafy gum trees line the verge
beneath a lazy blue sky.

At dusk, the earth resounds
with pounding feet
as mobs of kangaroos bound
among the gums and ancient grass trees.

Be quick to glimpse the joey
on koala mum's back
as she clambers from her tree
and toddles down the road
to extinction.

Lindy Warrell

Deception

We bathe in a rose's perfume
oblivious to its thorns
we know a snake's venom
and lust for his beautiful skin
to make a poisonous purse
for secrets.

Nor love be innocent
in messages of varying intent
cloaked by a tight smile
and false heart
to culminate
in black eyes and bruises.

In words, utterances fly
but sweet to an innocent ear
is the dart that kills.

A Curious Mix in Free Verse

An Unquiet Garden

A common blackbird
splashes in the bird bath
yellow beak dipping
safe
hidden by a river gum's evergreen shade.

Sparrows hop in
honey eaters flutter, a thrush bathes
then pigeons descend; fat,
strutting, pouting, tail feathers fanned —
wings lifted in warning.

Murray magpies scream black and white
raucous in their nest
a young kestrel below clasps their chick
alert
taut on one leg for escape.

Lindy Warrell

As For Cats, Least Said...

Men are just fine
  no need for money or looks
  just sunshine in their hearts.
But husbands are not so special
  some are dangerous types
  who bruise and occasionally cheat.

Women — Ah! Women.
  Their shapes, smells, smiles
  and winsome eyes are wicked perfection.
But wives in pinnies are pretty plain
  useful for wiping bums
  of kids who suck thumbs.

Babies are sweet little things,
  when they sleep all night
  and are all a-plump with giggles.
But human offspring are
  scary teens who damn you
  and never say why.

Dogs. Well, dogs are easily led by kindness
  to salivate, lick and plead to be fed
  before bed. Your bed.
Yes, our canine friend is an obedient brute
  but it sheds fur and pisses
  on the floor in front of the door

As for cats…

A Curious Mix in Free Verse

Giving or Taking?

Malice in a poisoned chalice
or shiny jealousy in red heart wrapping?
What is a gift if not an unspoken web of expectations?
Of love, perhaps? Gratitude springs to mind. Obeisance?
Maybe —
for chocolates and wine. But dog minding, childcare,
and hospital visits demand to be met in kind.

What do we say, then, of flowers?
Those gratuitous plucks from nature
we secretly watch wilt unwatered in the hot afternoon sun
or force, still wrapped in foil and tied with a silk ribbon
into a bin. Surely those unwanted stalks
sticking upward tell the tale.

A friend, kind to your husband on his birthday
now there's another dimension
one we often forget to mention
she's so sweet, we say and look the other way
as good manners demand
then we find her man and take *his* hand.

Lindy Warrell

Along the Way

I saw you sitting there
cross-legged like a Buddha
your back to the trunk
of a gnarled old tree
awaiting enlightenment.

I blinked
and you were gone.

A Curious Mix in Free Verse

A Tale of Two Trees

Between delivery truck vibrations
and ambulance whines
rainbow lorikeets gossip
and roost in Norfolk Island pines
embedded in concrete
far from home
inhaling acrid fumes.

Across the way, tender branches
of young gingkoes are skyward bent
in answer to dying pines,
a tree with no family; a fossil
with fan-shaped leaves, smelly fruit
and medicinal nuts tough enough
to thrive.

Flush and shady or deciduously bare
the hardy gingko hosts few pests.
We may ingest its Biloba healing
but native birds and creatures
find no home in this pretty maidenhair.

Lindy Warrell

Damaged Goods

Blonde, blue-eyed,
lipstick smiles
to hide the pain
of beatings,
bruises, cracked skull
months of treatment
diminished capacity
left to raise three babies
alone —
she wants to write a blog
but who wants to read
such misery?

Brown eyes, black hair
wavy silver streaks
bobby-pin flowers
pink silk ribbons
neck swathed in lace
from jawline to clavicle
over memories
of failed strangulation
etched forever
in the blood spots and madness in her eyes —
her children ran away
ashamed.

A Curious Mix in Free Verse

Red hair, hazel eyes
freckled face
plump
giggling outside a club
with friends and a false ID
raped at 13
drugged, discarded on wet pavement —
pregnant to evil
she raises her baby in isolation
on a government pittance
reporting to bureaucrats
as though she did wrong.

White hair, dyed hair
eyes dimmed by age
faces wrinkled in pain
black, brown, yellow, pink,
masked by smiles, makeup or niqab –
old women, wise women
who raised daughters
to be loving and strong
sons to be honourable
at home as at war:
in every generation,
damaged goods

Lindy Warrell

Deconstruction

Old lyrics
icons of belonging
irrelevant riffs
in ageing memory.

Words, disengaged
from soils, families and cultures,
rootless hearts
in exile.

Walk three paces and
inextricable seconds pass.
Travel hemispheres,
cross foreign borders…

…and, boom!
Darkness descends.

A Curious Mix in Free Verse

Desk Magic

I love my desk
its smooth surface
like a secret
waiting for words
reluctant to come.

Instead, ornaments,
the internet
email and phone
fill and colour
the white space
beside books on
Buddhism, poetry, and
how to write, and
I cruise the web
till my mind comes adrift
on a sea of nonsense
that goes nowhere.

So, I dust, and I polish
I rearrange
and wipe the computer screen
until this beauty
my desk, my magical realm
seduces swirls of imagination
into poesy.

Lindy Warrell

At My Place

Through open louvres
our verandah of humidity
reaches for the fruit
of prickly palms.

We were young once
you and I, barefoot
and happy but
our bed is empty now.

Tears burn my throat
my stomach writhes
with the memory —
bombed bliss.

A Curious Mix in Free Verse

It Starts with Pink and Blue

Seagulls screech
over a fatty salted chip
cast by a little girl with palms up
longing to stroke their feathers.

A small boy alone with his dad
chases the birds, roaring
to shoo them away
waving little tough-guy arms.

He pokes his tongue out at the girl
who hides her face
in mother's skirt,
peeking out with curiosity.

Lindy Warrell

Kintsugi

fading from sight
white hair, pale skin
bloodless lips and a body
shrinking —
as the therapist asks about
age, profession, partner
parents, children, siblings,
delicate jigsaw pieces
resurrect a portrait
in glorious colour
traced with fine golden lines
of life's fragility

A Curious Mix in Free Verse

Iso in the City

A thousand eyes gaze
through black windows
on high-rise apartment blocks.
Inner emptiness screams
across the skyline.
Automatons move from bed
to breakfast to bathroom
to work and back to the TV.

In the city, blackened windscreens
clam tight against sun, smog and fear
the fun of fresh air forgotten,
as warm bodies grow cold.

Lindy Warrell

The Shame

I get mad very mad you guessed it I am cross and angry and pissed-off not to speak of beside myself whenever I hear about you know rape that thing men force onto women who don't want it who say no but men don't get it they do not understand the English language and the meaning of words like no go away bugger off or stop which is a red word but do you think it makes a difference of course not it seems to attract like a rag to a bull in a china shop whatever that means but they do say not to wear red around a bull so perhaps if we say go for it mate in green it might scare them half to hell after all if they are not taking perhaps they'll find they didn't want it in the first place that v-jay-jay that lovely sacred soft spot in a woman that can be so inviting to those who are welcome you often wonder don't you if he'll be perfumed or gross but when you want him it doesn't matter and when you don't it's all the fucking same full of shame not his but yours why's that do you reckon?

A Curious Mix in Free Verse

Emergency

You wait long
to be treated
overworked staff
smile past your gurney
unaware that your stomach twists
in pain
towards the aroma of
meals served to others.

Invisible, you release
an unashamed fart
behind the curtain.

Are you alright, dear?

Lindy Warrell

Lazy Afternoons

on my tummy across the bed
pillow for a bookrest
I escape into a dance
of insanity and love

characters undaunted
catch my heart
take my breath away
I yearn

for the wordsmith
whose tales
bewitch my mind
enrapture me —

make me

A Curious Mix in Free Verse

Natural Selection?

The world I once knew
is jagged with new bits
that outshine flab and shabby
with toned bodies
protruding breasts
and pouty puffed lips
to match eyebrows lifted
in perpetual astonishment
by the science of eternal youth.

Wrinkles, crinkles, and blotches
gnarled hands and sagging tits
no longer tell their tales.

We'd probably die out
if we were potatoes.

Lindy Warrell

Looking back

In an office of optimism,
the world stopped to watch men
on the moon
on black and white TV,
a small box brought from home
with cupcakes,
curried egg and cucumber sandwiches
by a secretary anxious to please.

The moon that sang blues
to girls with broken dreams,
and your Buddha glow from
sun's refracted light
were pushed from your beautiful face
as opportunity took its place
in a rocket shot past twinkling stars.

That's one small step for man,
one giant leap for mankind.

Fifteen minutes it took on TV
maybe twenty and she
was left alone with the mess
as men in offices everywhere
returned to plans and pens.

A Curious Mix in Free Verse

An Undecided Sky

As I emerged from hibernation
to stroll the pier in the sun
a furious sky moved fast and free
framing clouds that formed, and as they ran
chasing one another transforming
between bands of blue above and below —
one minute I saw a gleaming warrior helmet
the next a divine chicken, then poof,
the sky turned grey.

Lindy Warrell

Here I Am

I have fallen in love with Myself.
Not me, Myself —
that person I wished I could be
when I was 12 up our mulberry tree
imagining what life would be
when I grew up.

Somehow me got lost,
in roles that piled up,
like mothering, working
and loving in a made-up world
acting as Myself for others.

It was hard at first
but look at me now,
giddy with what my pretend Self gave,
a bounty of words to play with
in stories and poetry that remind me
I am one.

A Curious Mix in Free Verse

Making the Bed

Sheets
white on white
quilt peeled back
from the warm spot
where lay a body
turning, sleeping,
snoring.

Eyes open on a new day
squished pillows
plumped full
crinkled cotton smoothed,
edges tucked away
no tight corners.

Bed linen floats
in a swoosh of air
over traces of dreams
activities of night
breathing life into
today, tomorrow
forever.

Lindy Warrell

Keep Up Peeps

First it was the modem.
Its router worked just fine
but Skype gave the game away
when friends' faces pixilated
and froze in ugly shapes.

You still love them of course
your family and friends
but the distortions
reveal unthinkable potentialities.

Then it was the iPhone.
In truth it was my dressing gown
that spat it into the loo as I sat...
I fished it out but
rice couldn't do the trick.

Getting new devices
to sync with their forebears
is a distinct art of learning
to unlearn and keep up —
technology is in permanent flux.

Apps grow from 32 to 64 or more bits
and become obsolete like fridges,
washing machines, cars and computers
while new operating systems blossom

A Curious Mix in Free Verse

in a historical nano-second
where perpetual learning
may even hold Alzheimer's at bay...
...until somebody updates Dashlane
the password saviour, so it can't talk
to the operating system and everything
becomes unworkable.

Can we ever be safe again?

Lindy Warrell

Serious Nonsense

The red jarrah dining table
wafts orange oil from its shiny surface
into humidity as thick inside
as out the window where my lime tree
sags under pelting tropical rain.
As the earth saturates, the tree lowers
inch by quickening inch
until its emerald canopy
licks the lawn and its fruit
runs away with the moon.

Gone, too, the camel-coloured pair
of Californian chairs, too big for sitting,
too small for Goldilocks to sleep,
and the high-backed apple-velvet job,
begging for antimacassars. I settled
on an L-shaped piece in chocolate brown,
just right for the dog and me.

Then I lost my house and the dog,
with me down to a room or two,
my cream leather rocker took off,
preferring life as a feeding chair
and the burnt coral velvet
got too hard to bear, and now
I recline in ruby-leather,
just right...

...until paintings slip away
with rugs and books and other things
I can't remember.

A Curious Mix in Free Verse

My Poet

I get in the way of my poet
who's silent before I know it
I think and think
and try not to blink...

I stare outside
to forget, forget, forget myself
till my poet pops up
with the right words

it doesn't always work you see
but there's a lot to like about me, me, me

my façade for example
goes for a ramble
to all sorts of places
among all sorts of people
where it may well extrude by mouth
but lest we forget it ingests
by eye and ear and mind
just to feed my poet

Lindy Warrell

Navigation

It will be a clear day today
after a morning of oncoming headlights
blanketed by fog
under a grey-sheathed heaven.

None can see where we go
nor whence we come
but each knows a path
from house to tall building
through the maze of highways and byways
as the workday begins in neon light.

We leave no trace
in the mystery of the city.

A Curious Mix in Free Verse

Now You See It

Sun glances off my mirror
dances over the fruit bowl,
oranges, apples, lemons
and passionfruit glow.

The blind closes.
Whiskey and cigar smoke
draw close. I cower
as a hand reaches out.

We met on a white beach
swam young and free
in blue briny sea.
He gave the jewel
that tethered me
like a cow's nose ring
and broke me down.

I open the blind
but cannot see.
Where is the love
he promised?

Lindy Warrell

On Visits

You can't control the elements, dear
Nana used to say
to Mum who hung around
in a grizzle
when it drizzled on the day.

Nana opened coat pockets wide
for me to peek inside
Nothing there, she'd say
clasping hands to chest.
I had to choose left or right,
and on her palm there lay
a Violet Crumble or Peppermint Crisp
to my eternal delight.

And, on occasion, a Cherry Ripe.

What's that man of yours doing?
Nan would enquire of Mum,
not at the gee-gees, I hope.
I can't for the life of me
imagine how a bright girl like you
could end up with such a dope.

A Curious Mix in Free Verse

Old Age

This bag of bones
is me, this wrinkled skin
is not yet a shroud
yet when I call out
nobody heeds.

Sentient still
my heart is invisible
to small daily tortures
of dissolution before death.

My eyes scream
I am here
don't look away
don't let them say
what is good for me.

Lindy Warrell

Once Upon an Apple

Luscious, delicious, crunchy apple
green, yellow and taut red skin
crisp for teeth poised
to squirt ambrosial juice
into open mouths.

Oh, apple, you salivary gland seducer,
no wonder children offer your magic
to their teacher.

At school, apples absent
from lunch boxes
draw a start and a collective in-breath
of horror.

In a bowl, you shine
your nutritional beauty
into any home. Good people
live here.

But then, there's that story
about Adam, Eve,
and you, apple
with a wretched snake.

A Curious Mix in Free Verse

Red

anger blazes across town
every which way we turn
over orange burning
and jealous green
tinder points for rage
smoulder in hearts
that leap into flame
when red blocks our path
till we jump from the car
to pulp another's body
for relief.

Lindy Warrell

Over and Out

Lightning ignites
excitement, except
in people who don't like peas
who are very hard to please.

That much we know.

Does natural red hair
go orange
or become brassy
before turning white
like henna-heads?

Who cares?

I've decided waiting for death
is a waste of time
we can't see it coming
and we won't know when we'll go.
So, take it easy.

All we have to do is live.

A Curious Mix in Free Verse

Seduction

Memory disrupts synapses,
strangling hearts and arteries
that ache for blood enough
to whisper.

The stomach cramps and writhes,
enfeebled legs fail.

No knife here but fear, and yet

when paralysis is near,
gentle green tendrils embrace us
with tiny white flowers and,
in jasmine's fragrance,
we are seduced.

Lindy Warrell

Relentless

A willow weeps
over a dry creek bed
leaves crackle beneath my tread
but when the wind whispers —
too late — I succumb to fear
of the man who'd slit my throat
in a heartbeat
should he find me here.

Stones pierce my feet as I run.

A Curious Mix in Free Verse

Of Eucalypts Lost

Grey-green droops of slender leaves
spread habitat across this land
for bats, ringtails, koalas
and crawly creatures until
sacrificed forests became miles of tiles
for settler roofs and roads.

Farmers came, and miners,
whose baked fields and murky yields
silenced the birds' empyrean chorus,
starved fragile fungi, sunlight-fed
by clever, clever leaves
that turn skinny side up
to preserve moisture for a parched earth.

Alone on verges, leggy roots rage
in ripples beneath snakes of tar.
They disrupt foundations, topple monuments,
and when their branches drop in water-starved shock,
people say, *Oh*!
We must get rid of those trees.

Lindy Warrell

Relevance Deprivation

Like loose lips
my fingertips text busy people
who return a simple like.
I wish I had a life.

It no longer matters
who I bed
I want to keep my teeth
and licence till I'm dead.

I am that mad old woman
who smiles and talks to dogs
as quick-quick owners drag them by on leash.
Babies only get a smile, and I wonder why.

Yesterday I heard my words
uttered loud
and a little proud
as though it's all OK.

A Curious Mix in Free Verse

Oddments

Starched Petticoat
and Tight Jeans
went for a walk one day

said Tight Jeans
to Starched Petticoat
I wonder what it all means

try as it might
with every endeavour
Starched Petticoat could not explain

so Tight Jeans walked away
with nothing together but socks.

Lindy Warrell

Things

A crystal sphere
makes my heart ache
for its owner who died.
It glances at me
through a mystical glow
like his last Christmas gift
of Swarovski owls.

In a drawer, a Christening gift
ivory carved pendant
of Jesus in the manger.
Beside it, a blue-green Paua shell Tiki
from New Zealand,
a koala teddy from my nana
as real to me as the Velveteen Rabbit
and the hand-knitted golliwog
from the lady next door
who felt sorry for me.

Today, I like the gilt
glint of picture frames
and the way the sun
casts its rays through a clear Buddha statue
in the morning or ricochets
off gold leaf trim in the afternoon.

A Curious Mix in Free Verse

Sleep is a Faithless Lover

The warm breeze whispers
through my window
come back, come back,
as it bathes me in the night.
I stretch like a cat.

I see the poinciana tree ablaze
red flowers hovering
over a still green sea
while skies swirl purple
into glowering grey.

The cruel fingers of lost voices
pierce my heart
like lightning strobes
with the force of thunder
before rain.

I wake.

Lindy Warrell

Silence

Silence hovers among leaves
dancing to a breeze
that hides the muted voices
of those forever lost.

It is the secret of a dingo's howl
on starlit nights, a desert of cawing crows
in scorching sun, and the slip of a sled
in deep snow.

Within, silence is a brain hum
in ears that thrum to heart's drum —
vitality's
orchestral rhythm.

In the outside world
we bounce, one moment to the next
oscillating on a binary sound-scale
of likes and dislikes.

Music and birdsong — tick.
Politics and gunshot — cross.
Giggling babies — tick.
A sharp tongue — cross.

Unwitting, we spin in this web
of echoes, reverberations
and discernments
where peace is yet to be found.

A Curious Mix in Free Verse

Plucking Day

On my mini urban balcony
beside a potted ponytail
and a green tin frog on the wall
I sit to pluck three white hairs
from my chin.

In my magnifying mirror
hair is harder to see
in the sun than pores,
with a mind of their own those hairs
are as tough as young soldiers to snaffle
with tweezers.

Mum had not a hair on her face
that I can recall. *Did you, Mum?*
   Ah! I see one
      steady your hand old girl. Gotcha.
        One down, two to go.
I think Nana did though.
          Another, and another. Done.
        Oh dear, there are four.

Below, the traffic starts its roar,
somehow, I didn't hear it before.

Lindy Warrell

Company of Strangers

On and off the tram
myriad faces
prams, cases and
the practice of staying upright
in a crowd.

I pull my walking frame
close to my knees,
prams must pass.

Straphangers jerk
at stops and starts,
standing among strangers
a performance art
texting, talking, reading or
taking a sneaky look.

A large backpack on
someone's arse hits me
in the face
making rough way
to the door.

Cold beside me
in black shirt and jeans
angry tattoos peep
from collar and sleeves —

A Curious Mix in Free Verse

a death-white face
glowers at the floor.

I say 'good day'
he says 'thanks' and smiles
we chat for a while
and laugh as we reach the terminus.

Lindy Warrell

Spring

Green sprigs appear
like summer undies
on winter branches
and within a week
trees fully clothed
become habitat.

Newborn leaves
tantalise in the sun
their breezy rustle
an orchestra for birdsong
and I am bathed in shade
protected, for now.

A Curious Mix in Free Verse

Please Stop

A friend made me laugh today
his cheeky grin and wit
got right to it
till I doubled over
clutching the giggle-guts
I'd lost years ago.

You know the one where two girls
roll around under sheets
with torches
screaming painfully
at a hysterical finger
till someone's mother
puts a stop to it.

I implored my friend to desist
but he laughed as much as me
a tonic of energy
that lent a glint of lust
to old eyes as we carried on.

Lindy Warrell

Spent

From womb to cradle
playpen to garden
into the streets
all the way to school
petals of life gently open.

For a time we bloom
work
glow in the sunshine of love
till despair finds us
and colour fades.

Spent and grey
we turn back
from street to settee
over cups of tea
and long days
waiting for the call.

A Curious Mix in Free Verse

Stillness

Sunshine
is there no end to your capricious
delights and derangements?
My body aches for you
who set my young heart on fire
yet, I now yearn for the cool tranquillity
of softer light, a moonbeam upon my face
and stillness.

Lindy Warrell

Coastal Fragments

Dark clumps of seaweed line the beach
like a tidal jigsaw searching for completion.

Birds flock and shimmer into flight
as my footprints disappear in a wash of seafoam.

Wet salty paws scratch my leg for the ball,
doggy fur stinks of dead fish. I smile anyway.

Where children play in soft sand,
cuttlebones await caged beaks.

Above the dune, a sly glint of binoculars,
seeking sleek bikinied bodies.

Native grasses rustle in the wind, gagging
on fag ends and bottles from a heavy night.

A Curious Mix in Free Verse

Lost Words

I lost my poetry
was it ever there?
I hope to find it
my mind is bare.

Lost poetry, oh!
where shall I look
in my heart
or in a book?

Where do you hide
my dearest friend
shall I wait for you?
it cannot end.

I search and search
yet nothing is found
it seems so long
since you were around.

I look in the garden
and over the fence
into the future
life is immense.

Maybe, just maybe
words will come
when I'm once again able
to trust my tongue.

Lindy Warrell

Surrender

What is this mystery
issuing
in cries of love
and regret.

We laugh
to keep death at bay
strive
for eternal youth

yet bodies wither
and perish
where reason and science
cannot follow.

A Curious Mix in Free Verse

Freedom

After the shock, freedom
like being at home alone
as a child with a book
able to sprawl across your bed
for hours, meeting characters
on adventures, loving as if
to avoid heartbreak
but crying anyway.

With no one to answer to
no fear arises. No need to defend
or parry or sharpen the wit
to protect yourself. No. You
are alone and safe at last.

Who's bored? Not I, my imagination
frolics even as I sleep
enticing me to wake, to rise
to write
to create magic on the page
the real and the surreal
colliding in a voluptuous
chorus of life.

Stillness follows. Satiated
I smile, open my heart
and fall back to sleep.

Lindy Warrell

The Desert Lies

Mottled red and purple
your vast stony plains
tell ancient tales
revealed from deep
by sun, wind and time.

Your red wrinkled sandhills
expunge lizard tracks,
snake trails, traces of life
with every breeze
as though pristine.

But, under sky's blue intensity
and scorching eye of sun
your shiny stones and shimmering sands
hide grotesque massacres, killings
and extinctions —
an innocent palimpsest.

A Curious Mix in Free Verse

Batik Bong

Elephant batik
on a four-poster bed,
carved mahogany and cane
beribboned by
delicate netting.

Through open louvres
our veranda of humidity
reaches for the fruit
of prickly palms.

We were young once
you and I, barefoot
and happy but now
our bed is empty

Lindy Warrell

Startled

Birds in trees
chattering
startled, they soar
swoosh
then silence.

A Curious Mix in Free Verse

Wrong Killer

His back bent
over the steaming carcass —
a 'killer'
shot at daylight to be
gutted and skinned for meat.

He straightens, pushing back his Akubra
exposing the white forehead
it protects from the sun.

The cooling carcass lies
oozing blood into red dirt
invisible but for buzzing flies.

As the heat begins to rise
a calf wriggles in amniotic fluid.

Pungent silence.

Lindy Warrell

Smoke is Sublime

White smoke through a car window
smoker's lazy elbow poking out
an echo of forgotten pleasure,
that cigarette shared after food
or sex. Especially sex.

I practised smoking
under stairs in Dad's pubs
hiding at midnight, mimicking
wealthy racing men's women,
cigarettes aloft in slender holders
between bejewelled fingers,
red nails gleaming
arms and necks arched, just so.

In the morning, I emptied ashtrays
brimmed to overflowing
with stale tobacco
on precious lipstick-rimmed butts.

So far away, but that long ago,
we didn't know it'd kill us.
The puzzle is, we're gonna die
anyway.

A Curious Mix in Free Verse

The Last Sausage

Lost pillowslips
and sock thieves;
cracks in the mind —
healed neither
by sandalwood nor
frankincense —
statistics filed
into rooms in fear,
a mere sausage
and bread roll
to fill the soul —
no sauce, no spice
no visitor.

Lindy Warrell

Back Then

Once were nightclubs
grab-a-granny joints
full of mums of teens
all lippy and nail polish
plus cleavage to greet a man.

Do young men still gather
I wonder
at the bar at the back in the dark
one hand in a pocket
the other 'round a jar
lascivious eyes
seeking prey?

Does the music still play
fast to faster then slow
to slower at the end of the night
as bump moves to grind
to eventual climax —
bar closed.

I drove past the Inn today
an innocent white building
green plants in the sun
shady car park out back
yet I felt the warm bulge
of lust
as though it were yesterday.

A Curious Mix in Free Verse

They say it's the Arkaba these days
on the other side of town
where older mums (younger grannies)
are not so easily grabbed.

Cougars.

Lindy Warrell

Summer

There is heat in the air today
heralding a scorcher.
I glimpse lambs, calves, and alpaca cria
through green lines of re-growth
overseen
by dark stands of Norfolk Island pines,
their long shadows foreboding
on late spring's yellowing hills.

I pray fire stays away this year,
we are running out of houses to raze
koalas and kangaroos to incinerate
and sap to desiccate in blackened trees.

How do we assuage the Devil's rage
to save flowers, birds, and bees?

A Curious Mix in Free Verse

Legacy in Sepia

An old sepia photo, Kit
short and frumpy and Karl
tall in his best brown suit, standing
at their Glebe slum door
holding me
in a crocheted shawl
trailing proudly white to ground.

Nanna Sassen was blind
with a vice-like mind
a tiny woman who ruled a brood of 13
seven were hers and six Karl's,
deserving of high regard.

Her first husband Jack died at war
but her youngest, my dad
declaimed in mock horror
that her eyes looked funny
and she had no money
but plenty of favourites; not him.

At eleven, he ran away
and all he would say
no trace of a smile till his dying day was —
*my mother was never happy
unless she was miserable.*

Lindy Warrell

The Missionary Position

It's men in robes on top
as women march out loud
banners high.

It's men in power who spread the word
their disembodied rulings
bearing down upon us.

It's men casting godly votes
having their way while a young girl
is alone with a coat hanger.

Life in the shadows
covered in blood
will time ever heal us?

A Curious Mix in Free Verse

At This Moment

I am drawn to silence,
to the echo, not the sound
to vibrations,
not the music.

I am drawn to stillness.
Where faces did once
collide, collude and cajole,
peace now haunts my days.

I am drawn to space,
the in between of things,
like the pause between breaths
now inexorably long.

Lindy Warrell

My Telly Habit

TV they say with scorn —
I watch too much you see,
but let me reveal
its amazing appeal.

I don my PJs
to lounge in soft pink
where nobody cares
that my feet likely stink.

Curtains closed
I dim the lights
for lambent screen
on lonely nights.

My dog and me
on the settee
remote in hand
in Wonderland.

Colours, faces, places flash
volume way too high
as stories invade
and burdens fade.

The screen is the place
where I lose my face
in anonymous, vicarious
surrender.

A Curious Mix in Free Verse

Begone

Heavy with wrap-around comfort
svelte in its tactile charm
my forest-green velvet bedspread
soothes and quells
my bruised and hurting heart.

Held hostage thus, I dream of lakes,
parks, pines and larks
and marvel at jangling
birdsong among leaves
scintillating in sunshine.

With blue-sky resolve
I wait for anger's flame to die,
vow to hold still forever
beneath velvet's green weight
too frightened to breathe
lest sparks ignite, as they do,
again, and again and again.

Lindy Warrell

To Exist

A hollow presence
treads heavy
across town —
cars, buses, and trams
roar through unfelt pain —
a body untouched
by human hands
unseen
voice unheard
mind unreachable
thinking yet unthinkably alone
in an eerie city.

A Curious Mix in Free Verse

My First Husband

Lying flat on his back, sheet between legs
one bent like a dancer in pirouette
hairy and lithe on white
with black eyes glinting
above pouting lustful lips.

Don't be shy, he said sipping whiskey
my crotch in his hand
possession in his heart
I want to see all of you.

Mouth of smoke
and hot liquor breath
he pulled me down till
my gut squirmed,
this man, my husband.

He, so smart in a suit,
I, young and easily fooled
but when the bruising started
I left. Years later
we met in the street.
I always admired you,
he said.

Lindy Warrell

Sad Fact of Night

Sleep roams the earth
in colours that swirl into mists
over wild seas
and frozen wastes
that fade into humid air
where the past becomes
white palm-lined beaches
happy faces
and far off-places
till dawn creeps over the horizon
and we struggle to recollect.

A Curious Mix in Free Verse

Where Truth Lies

*I want the truth, the whole truth
and nothing but the truth*
thus spake my father,
upon his face, a grin
when mother scolded him
for leniency.

You're a good girl, he'd whisper
in my ear and wink
when poor Mother turned away.
She's at the end of her tether
that's what he'd say
when things didn't go his way.

He thinks of no one but himself,
in Mother's words,
*he's bloody selfish
like all men,* she'd say
and walk away.

I never found the truth
of what transpired between
this funny man, my dad
and the dour woman
he took to wife; except,
there was always strife.

I fear I'm more like Mum today
'cos the funny stuff wears thin.
Now there is the bloody truth.

Lindy Warrell

Waiting

Humidity hugs the earth
my body drips
for air
globules of sweat
form a patina
on my forehead
my hair is dank at the nape
moist clouds press down
heavier than my mood
torpor sets in
my skin sprouts anew with sweat
in battle with the lazy fan
swinging useless
from the ceiling.

Tomorrow's rain.

A Curious Mix in Free Verse

Till Wrinkles Come

Yellow doesn't suit me
I'm blonde
it makes me sallow.
My white skin, however, is comely in red
when I am golden ready.
Green also suits but
it emits that fallow signal.

Call me shallow if you wish
but a girl must know
her colours
and how to dress in jewels.

Gold takes my fancy
silver is for the table
while a lustrous pearl is the stuff
of fable for pale skin
a single beauty makes breasts
rise brazen from satin or silk.

If I were brown, I'd wear gold, pearls,
silk and satin, the whole manifold
plus the bindi of womanhood.
But a blonde must decorate her eyes
arch brows, add long, upcurling lashes
of childlike wonder
and paint full lips
to pout eternal like a baby.

Lindy Warrell

Trees

You cocoon me with strong trunks,
bathe me in whispering leaves
as I reverberate in the hallowed halo
of birdsong.

I rest in your gentle shade
alone but unafraid
and with returning strength
sway to your heavenly harmony.

As photosynthesis feeds you
ties you to earth
sun dapples my face
into a smile of welcome.

I am ready for what lies ahead.

A Curious Mix in Free Verse

To Wrack and Ruin

Lovely Lady
said to Beautiful Girl
what can we do about you
your brows pencil-thin
and monkey-bum lips
with all that injectable goo?

Beautiful Girl replied
Lovely Lady, well
I'll never look like you
your cheeks aquiver
with scraggly lines
and lippy leaking through.

Beautiful Girl and Lovely Lady
were once Dad's pride and joy,
when short, short skirts
or pinnies and perms
brought heartache to man and boy.

But when silicone gel
brought ageless breasts
men took up paper and pipe
to hide salacious thoughts
that cause
a gentleman's trousers to rise.

Lindy Warrell

Today's Poem

It is always today,
neither yesterday
nor tomorrow.
It is always now,
yet we journey to the past
or travel to a hoped-for future
seeking respite
in fond memories
or hope.
Such weightless images
bright and clear
belong to a heart
in pain,
only today, only now
is love.

A Curious Mix in Free Verse

Tourist Dreams

in coastal jungles
yearnings writhe
like vines on palms
along sandy shores…

we swim in crystal
seas so warm our bodies
glisten below
the blue surface, a shimmer
of black and white
entwined…

in ecstasy by night
we ride the stars
to the fragrance of frangipani
and a primal drumbeat.

Morning peels away
the illusion.

Who pays?

Lindy Warrell

Water Most Fowl

Feathers and down
live plucked
from ducks and geese
for our comfort.

Featherless wings
strive in vain to protect
ducklings and goslings
as they dabble —
camouflage down.

Long-necked geese get angry
flat-billed ducks are stout
(they dive more
and do not interbreed)
but on water, these feathered fowl
are most sociable friends.

We all know Donald and Daffy,
believe things that quack like a duck and
look like a duck, probably are ducks
but while we are game to gander
at forbidden things, we probably don't know
ducks mate for a season, geese for life.

Then there are humans
a species that breeds at large
dabbles in plastic
and builds nests of munitions,
camouflage up
with nary a feather or down.

A Curious Mix in Free Verse

Be Still

In liminal moments
listen intently,
there is no other thing to hear
but a pulsating impulse to story-fi.

In utterances,
nuanced for listening ears,
words connect as stories, like waves,
rising and falling away.

In silence
when we have no face,
jumbled words tumble onto the page,
tempting and exciting as good friends
begging us to go deeper
and deeper still, until
we cry at truth's beauty.

Lindy Warrell

Willy Wagtail

Above traffic's hum
between screeching Harleys
and freezer-truck deliveries
emitting their diesel fumes,
tiny claws alight on my balcony rail.
With darting looks and quick flicks of the tail
a small, feathered ball
all black and white
whistles his heart into mine
with tuneful notes
pure enough to pierce heartache
like a glint of sun
in winter's darkest clouds.
Where do you take my smile, willie wagtail
when you flit away?

A Curious Mix in Free Verse

Through Glass Blindly

Eyes like marble — blue, brown
hazel, green or grey
gaze through meniscus lens and
multifocals. Myopia
with or without prescription
blind to superficiality
in the gift of a diamond-cut vase
facets oblique enough to dash wedding dreams.

Twittering shy before the glowering
glow of a stained-glass window
two hearts seek to throb as one.

You may kiss the bride.
A toss of flowers, joy and laughter.

After the party
in a night-dark lane
booze-mizzled blood,
on sodden lace.

By morning all that remains
is a glasswashers' tale,
a frothy cacophony of
tumblers and beer glasses —
pony, butcher and schooner —
jostling cheerfully against
sturdy shots and elegant liqueurs
while top-shelf brandy balloons
flirt with champagne flutes
in an elegant tintinnabulation of lies.

Lindy Warrell

Who Nicked the Sun?

Banded together in a steel grey canopy
clouds ice up with their promise.
Hard rain.

We draw the curtains and
hunker into an inner journey
excavating remnants of the past
to sip and savour like mulled wine.

The sun's gone north for winter
a witty soul proclaims.

Seasons have a purpose
see how moods change
with the sky. Drab dark days
tempt us to snuggle or snooze.

But, in the gloom
and in the absence of company
the risk is that you'll confront yourself
full-on.

Illumination is right there.

A Curious Mix in Free Verse

Tinkle Time

What's wrong with you
you stuck up bitch
loud voice to audible whisper
then command — *Give us a beer*
if it's not too much trouble —
coins jingle in his pocket, hand
too close to the groin for innocence.

Give us a kiss, Luv, to a round of mirth
Nah, a beer'll do — If you've got the time —
always the barb.

Jees, another grizzles to mates
shoving coins at the barmaid
across the bar, *She's a miserable bitch,*
someone ought to give her one.

Time gentlemen please, the boss announces
to a good-natured groan from the crowd
while she took her pay and her tears
to a place she'd been many times before.

Lindy Warrell

The Time is Nigh

It's time to write a new poem
about - Oh! what could it be?
I thought of something a moment ago
but it just up and left me.

Bugger

Perhaps I'll write an old poem
in some other sort of guise
one that's been here earlier
refreshed as a big surprise.

Nah

What was that clever thought?
My mind is loose nowadays
slippery as all get-out
in people of my age.

Ahha

It nearly came, I almost caught it
but, again, it slid away
some silly nonsense I suspect —
they will tell me, won't they?

Hmmm

Perhaps the time is nigh
- *where is that ruddy nurse* —
I fear my lovely fleeting thoughts
may be forever lost to verse.

Acknowledgements

I started writing poetry in retirement. South Australia has the most amazing underground poetry scene where there are gigs almost any weekend or night of the week.

Ochre Coast Poets of Seaford was the first group to take me on as a rookie 15 years ago. Their critique taught me a lot, and I joined Friendly Street Poets, where I learned how to read poetry at a microphone where nobody threw rotten tomatoes and began to gain confidence.

I attended Fleurieu Poets in Goolwa hosted as an outreach of Friendly Street Poets by Nigel Ford. Two of my chapbooks were launched there to a welcoming crowd, one by Nigel and another by Jude Aquilina, whose wonderful Milang Poets gave rise to a number of the poems in this book.

When I moved to Glenelg, I founded TramsEnd Poets, a critique group that has survived nearly seven years. I have been a guest poet, workshop convenor and occasional visitor at Poets at the Pub in Gawler, where Veronica Cookson launched my third chapbook. And, until recently, I was active in Goolwa's writing group, Sand Writers.

I thank everyone from these groups for their insights, guidance, and friendship. It's not their fault my poems are curious.

'Of Eucalypts Lost' and 'The Desert Lies' were both first published in July 2022 on Steve Parish Nature Connect at https://www.steveparish-natureconnect.com.au/creative-life-lindy-warrells-word-journey/

Some poems in this collection may also be found on https://wattletales.com.au.

About the Author

Lindy Warrell is a novelist, blogger, and poet with a PhD in anthropology from The University of Adelaide. Her debut novel, *The Publican's Daughter*, was published in 2022. She has edited two poetry collections in collaboration, and her poems appear in three chapbooks, online and in literary journals.

A publican's daughter and mother of three, Lindy lived in Post-War Japan as a child, travelled in South Asia, did postgraduate field research in Sri Lanka, and has worked as an anthropologist across outback Australia. *A Curious Mix in Free Verse* is her first poetry collection.

Stay in touch with Lindy at
https://www.wattletales.com.au.

www.ingramcontent.com/pod-product-compliance
Lightning Source LLC
Chambersburg PA
CBHW070309010526
44107CB00056B/2537